THE LITTLE BOOK OF
MAN UNITED

Independent and Unofficial

SIXTH EDITION

EDITED BY
JUSTYN BARNES

First published by Carlton Books in 2001
Updated editions 2010, 2014, 2017, 2020

This edition published in 2023 by OH!
An Imprint of Welbeck Non-Fiction Limited,
part of Welbeck Publishing Group.
Based in London and Sydney.
www.welbeckpublishing.com

Compilation text © Welbeck Non-Fiction Limited 2022
Design © Welbeck Non-Fiction Limited 2022

A CIP catalogue record of this book is available from the British Library.

ISBN 978 1 91161 036 6

Printed in China

10 9 8 7 6 5 4 3 2 1

CONTENTS

INTRODUCTION

Football, someone said, is all about opinions.
And one club generates more opinions than most.
Whether it's in the media, the dressing room or in the
pub, Manchester United is frequently the topic of
conversation. Hardly surprising really, when you
consider that many of the game's most dramatic
events, finest players and greatest matches have
United at their core.

So here is a collection of some of the best soundbites
around, covering all that's legendary about the club –
the glory of the 1968 European Cup win, the class of
'92, the incomparable achievements of Sir Alex
Ferguson and the appointment of Ten Hag.

Best, Charlton, Giggsy, Becks, Keano, Cantona,
Rooney, Mata and now Rashford, Fernandez, Ronaldo
and Casemiro are all featured, along with the thoughts
of managers and a host of other legends from across
the decades. Whether it's to give praise or show
warming, jealousy or regret, everyone's talking
about United.

CHAPTER 1

THE UNITED WAY

" For men who work on the shop floor, the one highlight of their week is to go and watch football. Matt Busby used to say you should give that man something he can't do himself, something exciting. That's why Manchester United always play attacking football. **"**

SIR BOBBY CHARLTON

❝ I had always had a feeling that one day I would join United. I don't know whether it was wishful thinking or just a sixth sense about my destiny. **❞**

DENIS LAW

❝I'm in love with Manchester United. It is like finding a wife who has given me the perfect marriage.**❞**

ERIC CANTONA

"Fourteen years ago, on the day of a youth team match I'd go to the pub with my dad and brother to have chicken and chips in a basket. Nowadays, I wouldn't go near a chip even two days before a game!**"**

GARY NEVILLE

April 2006

❝My wife told me that I loved Manchester United more than her. I told her that I loved Manchester City more than her...**❞**

An unnamed **MEMBER OF THE CARRICKFERGUS BRANCH OF THE SUPPORTERS' CLUB**
explains why his marriage ended in divorce

❝At the end of the game you're knackered and there are times when you come out of the shower when you feel you can hardly walk. But if I came off the pitch and didn't feel like that, I'd feel as if I'd cheated myself by not running my hardest.**❞**

WAYNE ROONEY
on giving his all, 2006

"When I see the rain it isn't important to me now. If I go outside and it rains, I jog! I smile, I say, 'Welcome to England!' At first I would be angry, now I make a joke about it. When it rains, I dance!**"**

PATRICE EVRA

gets acclimatised to the Manchester weather, November 2006

❝ David Beckham and I were standing in the centre-circle when the crowd started calling me names. I said to him, 'I suppose you're used to all this.' He grinned and replied, 'Yeah, but in my case, it's not true!' **❞**

Referee **GRAHAM POLL**

15

❝I was beginning to get worried. I've never gone three seasons without winning the title before. **❞**

RYAN GIGGS

2007

"I was never fined for the Sharpey Shuffle, but the Boss threatened to. I said if he stopped me doing it I would stop scoring goals! **"**

LEE SHARPE's

unique goal celebrations didn't impress Alex Ferguson

❝I'm not one for falling over easily.
I'm not one for diving in the penalty box.
I don't think the team has ever got any
penalties from me.**❞**

United's very honest striker **ANDREW COLE**

❝My dad tells me that I've always wanted to play here. He said when I first saw Old Trafford I just stood and stared for an hour.**❞**

GARY NEVILLE

"I found it very difficult returning to Old Trafford for the first time. I got a marvellous reception, but the game just passed me by. Some of the Chelsea lads had a go at me after we scored. They reckoned I didn't jump up and down enough."

MARK HUGHES

❝I love pleasing United fans, but I also get a kick out of being on the pitch and having the power to aggravate thousands of opposing fans without them being able to do anything about it. **❞**

MARK HUGHES

"Here, it's all about the next challenge. No matter what we've done, no matter how big the game we've won, the boss just says we can celebrate what we've done to win a trophy – but the next day it's forgotten.**"**

Onwards and upwards for **NEMANJA VIDIC**
May 2008

❝ There's no amount of money that can buy the feeling we have now. We want more. We want to go past people who have been here before, we want to win two, three, if we can. That's what drives us on. **❞**

RIO FERDINAND

on United's desire for more Champions League glory, May 2009

❝We had fights, and I mean punch-ups, every day. But it didn't matter. We were men enough to take it and forget about it come kick-off time. It didn't matter whether Nobby had chinned Denis or Denis had chinned Bill Foulkes, we were all aiming for the same thing ultimately… **❞**

GEORGE BEST

"… and by matchday,
you had to be friends because
there was only one bath! **"**

GEORGE BEST

You go to any factory or office and not everyone is going to like each other. Of course, you are going to have clashes. It's not to say we won't have a good do at Christmas and come Saturday, we will all want to win and we will help each other out.

ROY KEANE

"As YTS players, we were all assigned to clean someone's boots. I got Eric Cantona which I was well pleased with … although Brian McClair was the biggest tipper!**"**

WES BROWN

"When you're in the tunnel and you hear on the speakers: 'Please welcome the champions of England, the champions of Europe and the champions of the world,' you just believe that you're going to crush anybody that is in your way. I get goosebumps every time I walk out at Old Trafford. **"**

DIMITAR BERBATOV

January 2009

❝ We are very proud to be shortly approaching a milestone 4,000th game featuring an Academy player, and we are particularly optimistic regarding the considerable young talent currently coming through. **❞**

ED WOODWARD

the United Chief Executive on the dividends paid by investing in the Academy

❝When I knew about the bid from United there was only one place I was going to go. The players here are unbelievable, the club has fans all over the world and hopefully I can do well. **❞**

WAYNE ROONEY

joins for £27million in summer 2004

❝You go into every single game at
Manchester United as a player or a manager,
thinking you're going to win. That's just the
nature of this club. The next one is always
the important one.**❞**

OLE GUNNAR SOLSKJAER

on the United philosophy when he became manager in 2019

"I think it's my time now. I knew we had to step up and kind of take charge. That's what I've done. The goals have come, which has given me confidence.**"**

JESSE LINGARD

on maturing as a player, January 2018

"Everyone who knows me, knows about my never-ending love for Manchester United. The years I spent in this club were absolutely amazing and the path we've made together is written in gold letters in the history of this great and amazing institution.**"**

CHRISTIANO RONALDO

on his return to Old Trafford, August 2021

" The chance to join Manchester United is a dream come true and I just cannot wait to perform in the Premier League. This is a young and exciting squad and I know, together, we can develop into something special to bring the success that the fans deserve. **"**

JADON SANCHO

after signing from Borussia Dortmund, July 2021

❝I've got very few words left for Manchester United. No anger, no comment anymore. They are a bit of a farce; you almost expect it from them. The players are taking Ralf Rangnick down with them. They are bad.**❞**

GARY NEVILLE

the former skipper spells out his frustration, April 2022

CHAPTER 2

HEROES OF THE SHIRT

❝Perhaps I should be an example to people, but I do not think that way, I do not react that way. I am simply me.**❞**

ERIC CANTONA

"I don't know about making referees professional. They love themselves enough as it is now.**"**

PAUL SCHOLES

❝I said many years ago the perfect partner for a striker is Wayne Rooney. He works not only for himself but for the striker and the whole team. I'm absolutely happy to be one of the guys beside him. **❞**

ZLATAN IBRAHIMOVIC

"Roy Keane is Damien, the devil incarnate off the film *The Omen*. He's evil. Even in training.**"**

RYAN GIGGS

❝I'm moody and grumpy
most of the time.**❞**

ROY KEANE

❝If I thought personal glory was more important than team glory, I would have taken up an individual sport. **❞**

ERIC CANTONA

❝It wasn't my choice to become a goalkeeper, but I was probably too violent to play outfield.**❞**

PETER SCHMEICHEL

"I train every day to be the best goalkeeper in the world, that is my aim. Schmeichel and Van der Sar were the greatest goalkeepers in the Premier League, they are legends for this club and that is what I want. **"**

DAVID DE GEA

❝ There's quite a few funny sights in the dressing room, but the thing that makes me happiest is Yorkie's smile. It makes everyone else smile too! **❞**

OLE GUNNAR SOLSKJAER

on the ray of sunshine that was his fellow striker Dwight Yorke

" In the changing room, Keaney would say, 'Watch this,' and he'd start humming or singing a song near Gary Pallister. Five minutes later, Pally would be singing the same song. It never failed, that one. **"**

RYAN GIGGS

47

“ It's a panic buy. **”**

Former Liverpool captain **EMLYN HUGHES**
when United bought Eric Cantona

It's not a case of signing autographs so that people will think I'm a nice guy, but rather that I don't want them to have a bad experience. I don't want to hurt them by letting them down.

ERIC CANTONA

"When you see Eric Cantona brushing up his skills, you know that no-one can be satisfied with their standard.**"**

RYAN GIGGS

❝He cannot kick with his left foot, he cannot head a ball, he cannot tackle and he doesn't score many goals. Apart from that he's all right.**❞**

GEORGE BEST

... on David Beckham!

❝ You shouldn't be nuts, but it doesn't matter if you are a bit peculiar. **❞**

PETER SCHMEICHEL

identifies the essential quality of a goalkeeper

"I'm sure Arsenal fans are working on some new chants, but they can sing what they like. I've got three nice medals to show them.**"**

Ex-Spurs striker **TEDDY SHERINGHAM**
looks forward to his next match against Arsenal in summer 1999 soon after winning the Treble

❝I play with a certain passion and fire.
I have to accept that sometimes this fire
does harm. **❞**

ERIC CANTONA

before the infamous kung-fu incident at Selhurst Park
in January 1995

“Rooney can be the best in the world at 25 if he knows you need to train hard, go to bed early and be careful what you eat. **”**

ERIC CANTONA

"Who am I more scared of – the gaffer or my missus? Neither. Always have your alibi ready – that's my motto!**"**

ROY KEANE

❝When I think football, I think Manchester United. I still support United and always will. I will die with them i n my heart. **❞**

ERIC CANTONA
2021

❝In 30 or 40 years time, I'll probably boast about having played with Eric… Even before I came to the club I looked up to him and admired his skills. And I admire him even more now after I've trained with him and got to know him as a person. He was a huge influence at the club and gave everybody a lift with his presence. That is probably what I'll miss most of all. **❞**

OLE GUNNAR SOLSKJAER

on hearing of Eric Cantona's retirement, summer 1997

"I think the fans appreciate my attitude, and I'd like to think there's no crap about me. What you see is what you get.**"**

ROY KEANE

"People have the image of me that I'm a bad boy. I'm this and I'm that. People are curious, 'How is Zlatan?' I'm a family guy. I'm taking care of my family, but when I come on the pitch I'm a lion. That's the big difference. I don't believe I'm arrogant.**"**

ZLATAN IBRAHIMOVIC

❝Nobody's going to tell me I'm the world's best, but no-one's going to tell me I'm a crap footballer either. I have belief in myself, simple as that. **❞**

TEDDY SHERINGHAM

"Teddy has always been a thinking man's player, like Franz Beckenbauer and Bobby Moore.**"**

GEORGE BEST

"My goal for this year is to become the complete striker.**"**

RUUD VAN NISTELROOY's

undemanding 2003 New Year's resolution!

"The variety of Van Nistelrooy's goals is incredible. If a cross comes in you know he'll be on the end of it, but he's also capable of picking the ball up 40 yards out and scoring. Phenomenal.**"**

GEORGE BEST

❝ To be honest, it was the balls. **❞**

MARCUS RASHFORD

downplays his magnificent "knuckleball" free-kick winner against Chelsea in October
2019, citing the lighter balls used in the Carabao Cup

❝Manchester United is a special and unique club because of its history. No one has won as many trophies as we have in the English league. That history is something you cannot buy. I think his club has a lot of great history and I feel very proud to be a part of it. **❞**

JUAN MATA

"You look around the Nike HQ and see people like Michael Jordan and Tiger Woods have buildings named after them. That's what I want – Ferdinand Towers in my honour! I want to join the legends.**"**

RIO FERDINAND

"The fans will be upset because they loved him. He was a great leader. The best thing about Roy Keane is that you knew where you stood with him.**"**

DAVID BECKHAM

on Roy Keane's departure from Old Trafford in November 2005

"You can learn more from the lows than the highs. The highs are great, but the lows make you really look at things in a different way and want to improve. Every player will have both in their careers, and I have, but what you get is that experience which is so important to perform at your best.**"**

WAYNE ROONEY

❝I'm very proud to have scored 100 goals for United.**❞**

RUUD VAN NISTELROOY

reaches his ton at Everton in February 2004, after just 131 games

❝After Philip left, I had half an hour to myself driving in my car and I did think: 'This isn't going to last forever. I'd better enjoy this.'**❞**

GARY NEVILLE

on life at Old Trafford after brother
Phil joined Everton in the summer of 2005

" Football is made up of all kinds of conflict. In a dressing room, between players, between us and the manager, between us and loads of people who don't seem to matter. It's constant and harsh sometimes. **"**

WAYNE ROONEY

"He started in 1992 and where are we now, 2009? Jesus. To play at the level he has been doing, he has to be the greatest ever player in the Premier League. Not just because of his longevity, but because he is still playing for Manchester United and still getting man-of-the-match awards.**"**

STEVE BRUCE

on Ryan Giggs, December 2009

"He has made a fantastic contribution to our season. In terms of impact he has had as big an impact as anyone I can imagine.**"**

SIR ALEX FERGUSON

on Robin van Persie's efforts during the 2012–13 season

❝Patrice is one of the finest leaders around the dressing room that I have ever seen. **❞**

DAVID MOYES

assesses Patrice Evra, December 2013

❝I wanted to go to a place where I would feel happy and I'm happy now. Manchester United are a massive club, with the most fans around the world so it's a big challenge for my career, a big step.**❞**

JUAN MATA

joins from Chelsea, January 2014

❝When you have to make a hard decision in your life, I always listen to that little boy inside me. What does he want? That boy was screaming for Manchester United. **❞**

ROBIN VAN PERSIE

explains why he left Arsenal

"It was the highlight of my career, playing for Man United and I was there for so long… I left with great memories… The fans have been brilliant to me.**"**

WAYNE ROONEY

United's all-time leading goalscorer admits he misses the club,
November 2018

"I will keep this shirt with me always.**"**

ANDER HERRERA

after his United debut in 2014

"I don't like to say myself I'm a leader. I give everything. I've always been talking, that's how I am, try to help the team as much as I can. **"**

PAUL POGBA

talks modestly about being seen as a leader in June 2019

The only thing I think about is helping the team, respecting all my team-mates, not being selfish.

JUAN MATA

gives further proof of why he is so respected across football,
November 2019

"As soon as you get the ball I am going to be in your face. You are not going to like it one bit. Are you ready for that because that's what's going to happen.**"**

DARREN FLETCHER

on his attitude in midfield

"It has been a privilege to spend eight years at this great club and the opportunity to continue my career at Manchester United is a genuine honour.**"**

DAVID DE GEA

after signing a new four-year contract with United in September 2019

"You can be a leader without being a captain. It's the way you live your life, how you are on the training ground, in your own life, how you grew up, your mentality, it's a little bit of all this.**"**

BRUNO FERNANDES

leading by example, 2020

"I don't have the education of a politician, many on Twitter have made that clear today, but I have a social education having lived through this and having spent time with the families and children most affected. These children matter... And as long as they don't have a voice they will have mine.**"**

MARCUS RASHFORD
campaigner, activist and United forward, 2020

"Manchester United is a club that has always had a special place in my heart, and I have been overwhelmed by all the messages I have received since the announcement on Friday. I cannot wait to play at Old Trafford in front of a full stadium and see all the fans again."

CRISTIANO RONALDO

on his return to Old Trafford, August 2021

“Thank you for your unconditional support through good days and bad days.**”**

BRUNO FERNANDES

the Portuguese playmaker's positive response to a challenging 2021/22 campaign

CHAPTER 3

GAFFER TALK

" As a player, I gave everything I had. Now walking out, leading the team, just being part of this team, it's very, very special.
We're playing for the supporters, we're playing for our pride, we're playing for the club's history. **"**

OLE GUNNAR SOLSKJAER

on the thrill of leading out the team at Old Trafford, February 2019

" When you look down the list of who you are going to get points off, you mark Manchester United down as zero. **"**

Derby County manager **JIM SMITH**

"You have to give Fergie credit.
He has brought United on leaps and
bounds… the bastard! **"**

Liverpool manager **ROY EVANS**

February 1998

"For the first year I was a pro, when the manager walked into the room I just shut up and sat up as if I was at school. If I heard him coming down the stairs, I would turn around and go back into the dressing room. I was definitely scared of him.**"**

PHIL NEVILLE

on Sir Alex Ferguson

ff People don't see him when he comes in and pinches our chocolates, or when he sings to us! The manager thinks he's got an excellent singing voice and well… we always agree with the manager. **JJ**

LYN LAFFIN

Sir Alex's P.A., relates another side to the gaffer's character

" Man United has to be in the Champions League. I think that the Champions League is empty when Man United is not there. Imagine the Champions League without Man United, Real Madrid, Barcelona. There are a certain numbers of clubs that make it not a Champions League without these clubs. That's Man United in their natural habitat. **"**

JOSE MOURINHO

"He treated my dad with a lot of respect
and always took time out for him.
I mean, little things are important to us and
Matt even remembered what sort of
sandwiches my dad liked. **"**

GEORGE BEST

on Sir Matt Busby

❝We had a few problems with the wee fella, but I prefer to remember his genius. **❞**

SIR MATT BUSBY

on George Best

"There are some managers that the last time they won a title was 10 years ago. Some of them, the last time was never. The last time I won the title was a year ago. So if I have a lot to prove, imagine the others.**"**

JOSE MOURINHO

2016

❝They should have brought
in the ten-yard rule years ago.
If Schmeichel was in goal and the ball was
moved forward because one of his
defenders was arguing with the referee, he'd
have come out and smacked them because
his goal's at threat. **❞**

GORDON STRACHAN

"Everybody now talks about Cantona being the main catalyst of United's latter-day glories. But without Bryan Robson, I maintain United might not have had the same stature when Eric arrived. Robson was the essence of United. **"**

RON ATKINSON

❝I asked Pep to phone me before he accepted an offer from another club but he didn't and wound up joining Bayern Munich in July 2013.**❞**

SIR ALEX FERGUSON

one call the Reds probably wished they'd received?

" This team never loses.
They just run out of time. **"**

United coach **STEVE McCLAREN**

" Unfortunately it was a very bad bottle of wine and he was complaining, so when we go to Old Trafford for the second leg, on my birthday, I will take a beautiful bottle of Portuguese wine. **"**

JOSE MOURINHO

on his post-match tipple with Sir Alex

“ I've got more respect for Ferguson than anyone else in the game. He is the master. He's like a Scouser, really. He's funny, and he even votes Labour. I love him. **”**

JAMIE CARRAGHER

September 2008

" Manchester United is the biggest club in this country. I know, you know, everybody knows. I am sorry. It is easy to know. "

JOSE MOURINHO

telling it the way it is

"The amount of big players wanting to join United is incredible. Maybe players want to go for the money to other clubs but if you ask them where they really want to be they want to wear the badge of Manchester United.**"**

DAVID MOYES

January 2014

❝I want to get it out there, I'm going to leave by the front door, because I think everyone knows I've given everything for this club. This club means everything to me and together we're a good match, but unfortunately, I couldn't get the results we needed and it's time for me to step aside.**❞**

OLE GUNNAR SOLSKJAER

the United legend calls time on his Old Trafford managerial career

" No, in medicine you would see this is an operation at the open heart, so there are more things to be changed than some little things here and some minor things there, and this is the good thing. **"**

RALPH RANGNICK

suggesting the Reds need major surgery, 2022

❝I am really excited to be here. It was a really warm welcome here in the club, and I am looking forward to working at this club… It gives me energy. I am looking forward to the new season, and today I feel quite well, I feel welcome. This is my home, and I want to achieve success.**❞**

TEN HAG

on joining, May 2022.

CHAPTER 4

INTO EUROPE

“Winning the European Cup in 1968 was a big thank you to the players that weren't with us, and even those of us who did survive. That night was something special. Everyone in the world wanted us to win at Wembley and doing so was part of the history – it was important the club managed it.**”**

SIR BOBBY CHARLTON

reflects on United's European Cup victory under Sir Matt Busby in 1968, March 2008

" We got the objective, we are back in the Champions League by winning a title, an important title. The club now has every title in world football. We fought hard for this since the beginning. "

JOSE MOURINHO

celebrates United's 2–0 defeat of Ajax in the
2017 Europa League final

"I couldn't tell you which hotel we stayed at, whether we had a post-match banquet… it's just a blank. But the game itself, I can remember almost every kick. I was fortunate enough to score in the Final. I remember the ball being cleared and coming to me. And I knew I was going to score, I just knew.**"**

GEORGE BEST

on the 1968 European Cup Final victory

"I want our fans to be happy and for them to enjoy the experience of being at Old Trafford. I would appeal to them to just enjoy the performance we intend to put on for them.**"**

Opposing captain **FRANCESCO TOTTI**
shortly before his AS Roma side lost 7–1 in the
UEFA Champions League, April 2007

" It was an unbelievable night. I watched football as a kid and saw players go up to the Royal Box at Wembley and thought, 'What are they crying for?' But as soon as the final whistle went, I just sunk to my knees. I couldn't stop myself. **"**

RYAN GIGGS

on the 1999 UEFA Champions League Final win

"The last time I saw a person dance on a table was Giggsy after we won the European Cup. He fell off and everyone was a bit worried, but he just got straight back on the table and carried on!**"**

TEDDY SHERINGHAM

"" Teddy Sheringham did all the hard work for me and I just managed to get a toe on the ball to steer it in. I have never had a better feeling than that and I doubt I ever will. It'll take a couple of years to sink in. **""**

OLE GUNNAR SOLSKJAER

on scoring the winning the goal in the
1999 UEFA Champions League Final

❝Even though it was the last minute, I was quite calm. I just knew we'd score, I really did. And as soon as we equalised I knew that there was only one team that could win it. I could see that Munich were gone.**❞**

Suspended captain **ROY KEANE's**
view from the bench

❝When I went down on my knees
I strained my ligaments and I was
out for the whole summer.**❞**

OLE GUNNAR SOLSKJAER

*reveals the cost of his UEFA Champions League
Final-winning goal celebrations*

" At the end of this game, the European Cup will be only six feet away from you, and you'll not even able to touch it if we lose. And for many of you, that will be the closest you will ever get. Don't you dare come back in here without giving your all. **"**

SIR ALEX FERGUSON's

half-time team-talk during the 1999 UEFA Champions League Final against Bayern Munich

121

" February 6, 1958, was a black day in the history of Manchester United, but also for football in general. I'm proud to be a fan of Manchester United. People in England say, 'God save the Queen'. Today, I say, 'God save Manchester United.' **"**

BAYERN MUNICH CHAIRMAN

at the service to commemorate the Munich Tragedy,
February 2008

"Even today when I see archive films of Duncan Edwards it really upsets me. We'll never get over Munich. The mood in the city was ghastly… The whole country felt for the club. Even in the 1958 Cup Final, everyone was on Manchester United's side… a bit different from today. **"**

NORMAN WILLIAMS
United supporter

"We used to go here, there and everywhere in groups, loads of us. We went to Butlins together, as a youth side we had our first trip abroad to Switzerland together. We were pals, best pals… and then the crash happened.**"**

'Busby Babe' **WILF McGUINESS**,
who missed the fateful trip to Red Star Belgrade through injury

"I can still remember the first television pictures. Snow falling in the darkness, the flakes illuminated by camera lighting and the sudden burst of flashbulbs. Snow, twisted metal, seats which had been hurled from the aircraft, overcoats and odd shoes.**"**

TOM TYRRELL

sportswriter and United fan

❝I was having a shave in the kitchen when my wife shouted out from the front room, 'Have you heard the news?' I'd shaved half of my face, but I don't think I shaved the other half for three days. I was absolutely devastated.**❞**

HAROLD WOOD

club steward

❝It may seem odd but when I think of Manchester United I think of Roger Byrne, Duncan Edwards and Eddie Colman before the Munich aircrash, and of Harry Gregg, Bill Foulkes and Nobby Stiles afterwards. Best, Law and Crerand were replaceable somehow. They weren't the heart of the team.**❞**

SIR BOBBY CHARLTON

CHAPTER 5

MAGIC MOMENTS

"Sir Matt Busby came into the dressing room after we'd become champions. He said very little but his expression said it all. His beloved Manchester United were back on top.**"**

BRYAN ROBSON

on the end of the 26-year wait for a League Championship victory

❝I can't believe it, I actually scored!
My first goal in 90 League and cup games!
Strangely, Ole Gunnar Solskjaer had a
premonition I was going to do it.
He came up to me three times in the hour
before kick-off and said, 'You're going to
score today, Phil. Remember what I say.'
I just laughed. **❞**

PHIL NEVILLE

on his winning goal against Chelsea on 28 February 1998

“Well, I rose like a salmon at the far post, but Pally rose like a fresher salmon and towered above me, headed the ball at the keeper, the keeper fumbled, then I saw a sudden flash of brilliant red and leathered it into the roof of the net with my left foot sponsored by Diadora boots.**”**

DAVID MAY's

vivid description of his goal in United's 4–0 thrashing of Porto in March 1997

❝It got to the point where I just thought, 'I'm going to take everyone on.' And when I got through I just hit it as hard as I could. David Seaman got a lot of stick, but it really was the only place I could have put it to beat him.**❞**

RYAN GIGGS

describing his wonder goal in the 1999 FA Cup semi-final replay against Arsenal

"After the 1994 FA Cup Final, I just sank to the floor and all my emotions poured out. There were tears, I cried. But there's nothing wrong with that.**"**

PETER SCHMEICHEL

remembers United's 1994 Double triumph

"When the seagulls follow the trawler, it is because they think sardines will be thrown into the sea. Merci.**"**

ERIC CANTONA's

enigmatic utterance after his court case in March 1995

"The seagulls following the boat represent Cantona's fans and the press who are always pursuing him. The trawler is a symbol of the judicial system which almost incarcerated him. The sardines represent Cantona himself, and the other players, who feel they are products in the capitalist system and world of sport.**"**

French literature professor **RUFUS DOISNEAU**
offers an explanation

❝My lawyer wanted me to talk.
I could have said, 'The curtains are
pink but I love them.'**❞**

ERIC CANTONA

offers an alternative explanation

❝It got the team spirit going, that's for sure. He's come back from what I thought was a very severe punishment...I think a lot of players would like to do what Eric did. There's been a lot said about the bloke in the stand that night and, fair enough, maybe he didn't deserve a size 12 boot in the throat, but some fans are really bad. Anyway, Eric got his punishment, did his time and that's the end of it. **❞**

ROY KEANE

December 1996

" When a young kid that loves the club he is at, and loves the game he is playing, this is what you get. The excitement in Marcus's face after scoring against our rivals is exactly what a kid his age should look like. **"**

DAVID BECKHAM

on Marcus Rashford's winner against Manchester City, 2016

❝At the end of the game, Jose Mourinho literally turned around to the press box and told them, 'I am still the number one. Do not doubt me.'**❞**

PHIL NEVILLE
former United star watches Mourinho celebrate the
2017 Europa League win

"This is one of the biggest, if not the biggest, football clubs in the world and to be the record goalscorer, it's a proud moment for me. It is obviously a great achievement and it is a moment in my career which I am extremely proud of.**"**

WAYNE ROONEY

after eclipsing Sir Bobby Charlton's club record of 249 career goals for United in 2017

❝For pure ability and talent, player for player, this is the best United team I've played in. And it can get better. We are champions now and that gives you an extra bit of confidence.**❞**

RYAN GIGGS

looks ahead after winning his eighth Premiership winners' medal

"It's incredible. It's a really proud moment for me, to join such a big club, I'm really looking forward to it and I can't wait to get started now.**"**

HARRY MAGUIRE

on signing for United in August 2019

CHAPTER 6

FERGIE'S SAYINGS

❝The afternoon of 2 May 1993, when we were crowned the champions of England was the day I truly became the manager of Manchester United. Until that fancy bit of silverware was in our grasp, nothing could be taken for granted.**❞**

SIR ALEX FERGUSON

“Nicky Butt's a real Manchester boy. A bit of a scallywag. He comes from Gorton where it is said they take the pavements in of a night time.**”**

SIR ALEX FERGUSON

❝ If he's got a temperament, wait until he
sees my temperament. **❞**

SIR ALEX FERGUSON

wasn't frightened of Eric Cantona's reputation

when he signed him in November 1992

Some of the players call me 'Gaffer' … and when Gary Pallister wants to take a weekend off, he calls me 'God'!

SIR ALEX FERGUSON

December 1995

"I've sung every song in the world in the bath. I'm thinking of releasing a CD called *Singalong with Fergie!* **"**

SIR ALEX "PAVAROTTI" FERGUSON

❝The intense pride in their city has made a deep impression on me and I now regard myself as an adopted Mancunian.**❞**

SIR ALEX FERGUSON

on being awarded the Freedom of the City of Manchester

66 My wife's always saying, 'Why don't you grow up?' and I say, 'Why should I? I'm enjoying myself being silly and young!' **99**

SIR ALEX FERGUSON

❝Eric Cantona is the best prepared footballer I've ever had. He's first at the training ground, he does his own warm-up and then he does ours. He trains brilliantly and then he practises after training and he's the last to leave the car park, signing autographs. He's happy to do hospital visits whenever you ask him to do anything. He's a model pro, an absolute dream footballer.**❞**

SIR ALEX FERGUSON

❝Managing this club can become an obsession.**❞**

SIR ALEX FERGUSON

"I remember Viv Anderson saying to me
once: 'You're off your head being a manager.
I wouldn't be a manager in a million years.'
When he took the Barnsley job in 1993, his
first phone call was from me. I said:
'Welcome to the madhouse!'**"**

SIR ALEX FERGUSON

❝I don't think any player in the history of football will get the sentence he got – unless they had killed Bert Millichip's dog. **❞**

SIR ALEX FERGUSON
slams Eric Cantona's nine-month ban
(Millichip was Football Association Chairman at the time)

"How would I be without all this, please tell me? And my wife wouldn't let me retire. She kicks me out at seven every morning. She's quite a formidable person.**"**

SIR ALEX FERGUSON

doesn't consider retiring in 2008

❝Everyone has done so well, I'm beginning to dread picking the team.**❞**

SIR ALEX FERGUSON

ahead of the visit of Everton in January 2009

❝I've known David since he was 11 and it's been a pleasure to see him grow and develop into the player he has become. I wish him and his family every success in the future and thank him for his service to the club. **❞**

SIR ALEX FERGUSON

ffYes, we take terrible risks, but there's always a chance we'll win the match. **JJ**

SIR ALEX FERGUSON

April 2009

"This club has always had players who show their true colours when the going gets tough dating back to the era of Nobby Stiles, Paddy Crerand and Bobby Charlton through to players like Bryan Robson, Mark Hughes, Steve Bruce and on to today's crop of monsters! That is why Manchester United have had so much success.**"**

SIR ALEX FERGUSON

reflects on United's amazing 2002–03 Premiership title triumph

❝Roy Keane has been a fantastic servant for Manchester United. The best midfield player in the world of his generation, he is already one of the great figures in our club's illustrious history. **❞**

SIR ALEX FERGUSON

on Keano

❝His whole meaning of life is about Manchester United. **❞**

SIR ALEX FERGUSON

on captain Gary Neville

“Some believe the greatest courage in football is the courage to win the ball. The other kind of courage – and it's a moral courage – is the courage to keep the ball. That's what Ronaldo has. All the great players had it. Best had it, Charlton had it, Cantona. 'I'll take the kick, I'll take the injury. But I'll keep the ball. I'll beat the bully.'**”**

SIR ALEX FERGUSON

on Cristiano Ronaldo, October 2008

❝Football, eh! Bloody hell!**❞**

SIR ALEX FERGUSON

in the tunnel minutes after United's last-gasp
UEFA Champions League Final win in May 1999

❝I remember the first time I saw him. He was 13 and just floated over the ground like a cocker spaniel chasing a piece of silver paper in the wind. **❞**

SIR ALEX FERGUSON's

first impressions of Ryan Giggs

❝It's getting tickly now – squeaky-bum
time, I call it. **❞**

SIR ALEX FERGUSON

on the title run-in with Arsenal, 2003

❝My greatest challenge is not what is happening right at this moment, my greatest challenge was knocking Liverpool right off their perch. And you can print that. **❞**

SIR ALEX FERGUSON

on where his priorities lay, 2002

❝ Myths grow all the time. If I was to listen to the number of times I've thrown teacups then we've gone through some crockery in this place. It's completely exaggerated, but I don't like people arguing back with me. **❞**

SIR ALEX FERGUSON

on his notorious "hairdryer" treatment

169

If my parents were still alive, they would be very proud. They gave me a good start in life, the values that have driven me, and the confidence to believe in myself. **"**

SIR ALEX FERGUSON's

family roots

"Do you think I would enter into a contract with that mob? Absolutely no chance. I would not sell them a virus. That is a 'No' by the way. There is no agreement whatsoever between the clubs.**"**

SIR ALEX FERGUSON

on Real Madrid's attempts to buy Cristiano Ronaldo, December 2008

"Sometimes you have a noisy neighbour. You cannot do anything about that. They will always be noisy. You just have to get on with your life, put your television on and turn it up a bit louder. Today the players showed their form. That is the best answer of all.**"**

SIR ALEX FERGUSON

after beating City 4–3, September 2009

"It's City isn't it? They are a small club, with a small mentality. All they can talk about is Manchester United, that's all they've done and they can't get away from it. **"**

SIR ALEX FERGUSON

on Manchester City's Carlos Tevez poster

"Sometimes you look in a field and you see a cow and you think it's a better cow than the one you've got in your own field. It's a fact. Right? And it never really works out that way.**"**

SIR ALEX FERGUSON

on Wayne Rooney's transfer request, 2010

❝There obviously will be a point when I do quit and when it is I absolutely have no idea because I tried that, and it was an absolute disaster.**❞**

SIR ALEX FERGUSON
on retirement, 2010

❝ It'll take them a century to get to our level of history. **❞**

SIR ALEX FERGUSON

on Manchester City, May 2012

❝ The decision to retire is one that I have thought a great deal about and one that I have not taken lightly. It is the right time. **❞**

SIR ALEX FERGUSON

on retirement, May 2013

CHAPTER 7

THE GLORY
DAYS

" George Best has ice in his veins, warmth in his heart and timing and balance in his feet. **"**

DANNY BLANCHFLOWER

❝You could knock the worst pass ever to Sparky and he would rip people's necks off to get it. At the time he wouldn't make gestures to make you look stupid, but a while later he'd come up to you and say, 'If you give me another pass like that, I'll have yer!'**❞**

PAUL PARKER

on the "the best all-round footballer I played with" – Mark Hughes

" Over the years people called several players the new Duncan Edwards… first Dave Mackay, then Bryan Robson. But none of them came close. He was the only player who ever made me feel inferior. **"**

SIR BOBBY CHARLTON

❝The lads used to call me 'The Judge' because I sat on the bench so much. **❞**

LES SEALEY

"In my playing days, you had
confrontations but the whole team
didn't pile in with their handbags. I think
football's become a game of prima donnas.
I like watching rugby where players get stuck
into each other, but they just get up and get
on with it. **"**

GEORGE BEST

bemoans modern players' behaviour

"Even when we played Leyton
Orient away, there were 18,000 in the
ground and more locked out. The crowds
at home were great, but we really noticed
it away because each game was a sell-out.
That gave us a boost. It made us feel
everyone was pulling together.**"**

SAMMY McILROY

*on fans' support in the 1974–75 season when United
were promoted from Division Two*

❝ In Turin, Gentile was marking me and I remember trying to get a cross in and he just stood on my shin. Later on, I was waiting for a corner and Gentile pulled a hair from under my armpit. I'd never had that before. **❞**

Former United winger **STEVE COPPELL**
recalls his painful lesson in the Italian art of defending during
United's 1978 UEFA Cup tie against Juventus

❝Robbo was coming to the
end of his career when I joined United,
but I still got a sense of how important he
was at the club. He was a top player and just
to play with him towards the end of his
career was an honour.**❞**

ROY KEANE

on legendary midfielder Bryan Robson

❝ When we won the Premiership in 1999, Dwight Yorke lifted the trophy and the crown fell off. I was in the crowd and turned to a total stranger and said: 'Great! I'll have to get that fixed on Monday!' She looked at me as though I was a total madman. **❞**

Manchester United Museum curator **MARK WYLIE**

❝Anyone that witnessed what George could do on the pitch wished they could do the same. He made an immense contribution to the game, and enriched the lives of everyone that saw him play. It is a very sad day.**❞**

SIR BOBBY CHARLTON

marks the passing of George Best in November 2005

❝Everybody knows the history of Manchester United, the significance of the club around the world and what it means to its supporters. To represent United is an honour and I am ready to give everything to help the team achieve our ambitions.**❞**

CASEMIRO

on signing for United, August 2022

❝We can talk about technical but it's all about attitude. Now you see we bring the attitude. There was communication, there was a fighting spirit and especially there was a team, and you can see what they can achieve. Because they can f***ing play good football!**❞**

TEN HAG

speaking to Sky on its live broadcast immediately after the memorable victory over Liverpool, August 2022. He apologised for swearing.

❝I think to build up good things, sometimes you have to destroy a few things. So why not – new year, new life and I hope that Manchester United can be the level that the fans want. They deserve that.**❞**

CRISTIANO RONALDO

on how United must rise from the ashes of a disappointing period, 2022

192